Daniel Boone and the Cumberland Gap

CORNERSTONES OF FREEDOM™

SECOND SERIES

Andrew Santella

Children's Press
An Imprint of Scholastic Inc.
New York • Toronto • London • Auckland • Sydney
Mexico City • New Delhi • Hong Kong
Danbury, Connecticut

Photographs © 2002: Brown Brothers: 7 bottom; Corbis Images: 20 (Richard A. Cooke), 16 (Hulton-Deutsch Collection),29 (Kevin R. Morris), 14; Dembinsky Photo Assoc.: 8 top (Ed Kanze), 17 (Bill Lea), 8 bottom (Skip Moody); H. Armstrong Roberts, Inc./W. Talarowski: 9 left; Hulton Archive/Getty Images: 3 background, 5, 13, 22, 26, 45 left; Kentucky Historical Society: 9 right, 37, 42 left, 45 right; Missouri Historical Society: 9 center; North Wind Picture Archives: 4 (N. Carter), cover top and bottom, 6 bottom, 10, 11, 23, 39, 44 bottom right; Peter Arnold Inc./Lynn Rogers: 19; Stock Montage, Inc.: 7 inset, 24, 27, 44 bottom left; Superstock, Inc.: 41 (Stock Montage), 12, 31, 44 top, 45 center; The Filson Club Historical Society, Louisville, KY.: 6 top (Daniel Boone Papers), 34, 42 right; Washington University Gallery of Art, St. Louis: 30 (*Daniel Boone Escorting Settlers through the Cumberland Gap*, George Caleb Bingham, 1851-52. Oil on canvas, 36 1/2 x 50 1/4 in. Gift of Nathaniel Phillips, 1890), 32 (*Capture of the Daughters of D. Boone and Callaway by the Indians*, Karl Bodmer, 1852. Lithograph, 17 1/16 x 22 1/8 in. Transfer from Special Collections, Olin Library, 1988), 33 *(Deliverance of the Daughters of D. Boone and Callaway*, Karl Bodmer, 1852, Lithograph, 16 7/8 x 23 in. Special Collections, Olin Library, 1988).

XNR Productions: Maps on pages 28, 40

Library of Congress Cataloging-in-Publication Data

Santella, Andrew.
    Daniel Boone and the Cumberland Gap/Andrew Santella
        p. cm. — (Cornerstones of freedom. Second series)
    Summary: A biography of Daniel Boone, focusing on his efforts
as a pioneer and trailblazer during America's westward expansion.
Includes bibliographical references and index.
        ISBN-13: 978-0-516-22526-5 (lib. bdg.)   978-0-531-18687-9 (pbk.)
        ISBN-10: 0-516-22526-X (lib. bdg.)   0-531-18687-3 (pbk.)
        1. Boone, Daniel, 1734-1820—Juvenile literature. 2. Pioneers—
Kentucky—Biography—Juvenile literature. 3. Explorers—Kentucky—
Biography—Juvenile literature. 4. Frontier and pioneer life—Kentucky—
Juvenile literature. 5. Kentucky—Discovery and exploration—Juvenile
literature. 6. Cumberland Gap (Ky. and Va.)—Discovery and exploration—
Juvenile literature. 7. Kentucky—Biography—Juvenile
literature. [1. Boone, Daniel, 1734-1820. 2. Pioneers. 3. Frontier and
pioneer life.] I. Title. II. Series.
F454.B66 S28 2002
976.9'02'092—dc21   2002001645

2 3 4 5 6 7 8 9 10 R 17 16 15 14 13 12 11 10 09 08

IN THE SPRING OF 1775, A GROUP of about thirty frontiersmen set off across the Appalachian Mountains. They traveled on old paths trampled flat by buffaloes and on narrow trails blazed by Native American hunters. The job of the thirty frontiersmen was to turn those trails into a road for **settlers**. To build the road, they hacked away at vines and branches and filled in huge holes so that wagons could cross. Their leader was Daniel Boone, and the road they cut was called the Wilderness Road. It led from Virginia through a gap in the mountains into Kentucky. In the early years of the United States, countless settlers followed the Wilderness Road to new lives in the West.

Daniel Boone helped
turn the Wilderness
Road into a route for
settlers heading west.

Daniel Boone, one of America's first great **trailblazers**, helped push the American frontier westward. Boone and his family were among the first white settlers of Kentucky. He founded two towns in Kentucky, Boonesborough and Boone's Station, and he led the defense of the new Kentucky settlements during the Revolutionary War. His adventures made him a hero to the thousands of Americans who moved westward in the 1800s.

THE BOONE FAMILY

Daniel Boone's father was a **weaver** named Squire Boone. He was a member of a religious group called the Society of Friends, or Quakers, who came to America from England in 1713 to avoid **persecution**. Squire Boone settled near Philadelphia, where many Quakers had made their homes. He married Sarah Morgan in 1720, and the couple started a small farm. They raised **livestock** and enough crops to feed their growing family. Just before Daniel was born, the family moved to a beautiful valley along the Schuylkill River. The Boones' new home was in an area called Oley, near present-day Reading, Pennsylvania. This was open country, at the western edge of European settlement. Here Squire Boone began clearing fields for a larger farm. He also built a one-room log cabin for his family. Daniel Boone was born in this log cabin on October 22, 1734. He was the sixth of eleven children born to Squire and Sarah Boone.

An early Quaker meetinghouse

5

THE SOCIETY OF FRIENDS

Many members of the Society of Friends settled in Pennsylvania because that colony offered them the opportunity to worship without fear of persecution. Pennsylvania was founded in 1681 by a Quaker named William Penn.

★ ★ ★ ★

As a boy, Daniel helped his mother tend to the crops and farm animals. The family kept chickens and a herd of dairy cows. Daniel often helped his mother drive the herd to a lush meadow a few miles from their house. Boone later said his love for the

William Penn(left) and other Quakers enjoyed good relations with local Native Americans.

6

Do hereby Certify that the Bearer hereof James McCushin Served as a Solder 2 Days in that part of the millitia of fin Castle at fort natton and Blackemores fort and was Ragelerby Discharge Certified under my hand this 25 Day of November 1774

Daniel Boone

Daniel Boone's education came in handy when he was older, as he had to write many notices of discharge for the men in his militia.

wilderness came from "being a **herdsman** and thus being so much in the woods" when he was a boy.

Tending to the family farm didn't leave much time for formal schooling. Boone himself admitted that he never attended a day of school in his life. However, he did learn to read and write as well as most men on the frontier. He also received another kind of education as a boy. From local woodsmen, Daniel learned the skills of a hunter. By the time he was a teenager, he was known as one of the best hunters in Oley. Hunting was important to the lives of settlers in the area around the Boones' home.

Daniel Boone grew up in a beautiful valley along the Schuylkill River.

The skins of animals such as beaver and deer were as valuable as money to frontier settlers.

LEARNING TO HUNT

Many of the settlers came from places in Europe where only the wealthy were allowed to hunt. In America, they found forests filled with game. A skilled hunter could provide meat to feed his family and hides to clothe them. He could also trade beaver **pelts** and deer skins for much-needed supplies such as gunpowder.

Hunters like Daniel Boone learned much from Native American traditions. Native American villages flourished near the Boone home, and relations between Native Americans and Quakers in the area were friendly. For the most part the Quakers of Pennsylvania and the Native Americans of the Iroquois Confederacy tried to avoid warfare. Daniel Boone's relatives were known as friends of the local Native Americans. Daniel even

DANIEL BOONE'S RIFLE

The hunter's most important tool was his rifle. German gunsmiths in Pennsylvania began making a new kind of rifle in the early 1700s. It was made especially for hunting, and it enabled a skilled hunter to hit a target 200 yards away. This weapon came to be called the long rifle because of its long barrel. Daniel Boone became a deadly marksman with the long rifle.

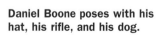

Daniel Boone poses with his hat, his rifle, and his dog.

This man is dressed in the type of frontier clothes that men of Daniel Boone's time wore.

★ ★ ★ ★

Daniel Boone dressed
in a beaver cap and
deerskin moccasins.

* * * *

learned to dress in a style that combined European and Native American traditions. He took to wearing a beaver cap, deerskin moccasins, a long hunting shirt, and a **breechclout** and leggings. As he approached adulthood, Daniel became more and more skilled in the ways of the woods. By the time he was fifteen, he had learned most of the hunting skills he would use for the rest of his life.

Iroquois Indians, shown here, were friendly with the Quakers in Pennsylvania.

Settlers, such as the Boone family, moved west in covered wagons.

LEAVING PENNSYLVANIA

In 1748, Daniel's father had a disagreement with the leaders of the local Quaker community. Three of the Boone children had married people who were not members of the Society of Friends. Quaker leaders disapproved of this practice, but Daniel's father refused to hear their protests. He left the church and began looking for a new place to live. He decided to move to the Yadkin Valley in western North Carolina, where good land was available at bargain rates.

The entire Boone family now headed south. The group included Daniel, his parents, his seven unmarried brothers and sisters, his two married brothers and their wives, and his married sister and her husband. They traveled in

Conestoga wagons, which were a type of wagon covered with a canvas canopy. The going was very slow because they had to make their way over roads that were very bumpy and sometimes dangerous. At times they had to stop because the roads were too muddy to travel or because fallen trees blocked their way. Making their way in this painfully slow manner, the family finally settled in Rowan County, North Carolina by 1751.

Around the same time, Daniel began going on long hunting trips to the West. He and other hunters used the same land that Native Americans had come to think of as their hunting grounds. When the supply of **game** began to thin out, the

Shawnee warriors in battle with U.S. troops

★ ★ ★ ★

Native Americans and white hunters came into conflict. All along the Appalachian Mountains, Native American tribes began to attack white hunters and white settlers. In 1753, Shawnee warriors struck not far from Daniel's new home in North Carolina.

WAR WITH FRANCE

Around this time France and Great Britain began fighting for control of North America. The French made allies of many Native American nations and encouraged them to

A battle scene from the French and Indian War

attack settlements in Britain's colonies. The British organized an army to drive away the French and their Native American allies. Like many American colonists, Boone joined the British in their fight with France. (The colonists were still subjects of the British crown.) In 1755, Boone enlisted in a North Carolina unit that became part of the British invasion force. He was made a wagon driver, and given the exhausting task of handling the teams of horses and huge wagons that carried the army's supplies.

That summer Boone saw his first combat. The army of British soldiers and their colonial American subjects were headed for Fort Duquesne, located at the site of present-day Pittsburgh. The French and their Native American allies attacked them at the Battle of Monongahela. The British remained out in the open in neat rows, which made them easy targets. The Native Americans used the cover of the dense forest, firing at the British from behind trees and rocks. The French and Native Americans easily defeated the British and colonial army.

Boone survived that bloody loss. The war between Britain and France dragged on for eight years. On the frontier of North America, French-supplied Native Americans continued to attack American settlements. Eventually, however, the British defeated the French. That victory opened the way for settlers to move westward. Daniel Boone would one day lead that move west.

THE FRENCH AND INDIAN WAR

The war between France and Great Britain was fought not only in North America. Both France and Great Britain had colonies all over the world, and the two countries fought the war all over the world. The part of the war fought in North America is usually called the French and Indian War. It was so named because it matched the British against the French and their Native American allies. The ultimate defeat of France by Great Britain ended French control of Canada.

A Cherokee Indian

STARTING A FAMILY

Back at the Boone home in North Carolina, Daniel met a young woman named Rebecca Bryan. The two married on August 14, 1756. Their first child, James, was born on May 3, 1757. Around the same time the newlyweds moved to a new home near present-day Farmington, North Carolina. Boone built a new house there, complete with a huge fireplace and stone chimney. It would be the Boones' home for the next ten years.

These were dangerous times for settlers in isolated homes. Many wars erupted with the Native Americans, and every so often, Cherokee or Shawnee raiding parties would sweep down on western North Carolina. The families of farmers would rush to take cover in nearby forts. Through all of it, Boone continued his hunting, going deep into the Blue Ridge Mountains and beyond in search of good hunting grounds. He hunted where today's states of Virginia, North Carolina, and Tennessee meet, roaming widely to satisfy his curiosity about the area. He hunted for months at a time and came to know this territory as well as any white man. He made friends with Cherokee people who also hunted in the area.

With Boone away on his long hunts, Rebecca had her hands full taking care of their family. By 1766 the Boones had produced five children and were raising another two children of relatives. In all the Boones adopted six motherless children of Rebecca's widowed brother. Boone was seldom home, and when he did return home, he found the

* * * *

neighborhood becoming too crowded. Western North Carolina was growing rapidly, with settlers moving in from all over Britain's colonies. All these newcomers cut into the supply of game that Boone depended on for his living. As a result, he began thinking about another move.

The Blue Ridge Mountains, where Boone went to hunt

In 1765, Boone explored parts of the area that is now the state of Florida, but he decided not to move there. Instead, in 1766 the family moved sixty-five miles west. Their new home was closer to the mountains of western North Carolina and to Boone's favorite Blue Ridge hunting grounds. He began taking his oldest son, James, along on his hunting trips. In the fall of 1767, they crossed the Appalachian ridge and descended into a land that was new to them. For the first time, Daniel Boone set foot in what came to be called Kentucky.

KENTUCKY

Daniel Boone was not the first person of European descent to enter Kentucky. Hunters and trappers had been going there for years. Traders from Virginia and Pennsylvania already made regular visits to Native American villages there. Still, white settlers had not yet made their way into Kentucky. Families had not moved there to live because the Appalachian Mountains stood in their way. Native American attacks discouraged anyone who considered moving there. Even the British government discouraged its colonists from moving west of the mountains.

Boone remained curious about Kentucky. On his first trip there, he barely made it out of the foothills of the Appalachians. Trapped in a snowstorm, he was stranded for weeks and was not able to return home until the following spring. The hunting was good, however. Boone hunted buffalo for the first time. He found an abundance, or large supply, of bears. It was enough to convince him that his future lay in Kentucky. In addition to the increasing number of people in

**LEARNING ABOUT
A NEW LAND**

When Boone was serving in the army during the French and Indian War, he heard stories about Kentucky. It was described as a beautiful land, overflowing with game. In fact, it was said to be a hunter's paradise. Its name probably came from the Iroquois Indian word *Kanta-ke*, which means meadows.

A black bear, much like the ones Boone saw in Kentucky

The White Rocks area of the Appalachian Mountains

North Carolina, Boone's family was expanding and his sons would need land of their own. He resolved to return to Kentucky someday.

He did return, and not just for a short visit. Boone spent a full two years hunting and exploring in Kentucky. Between 1769 and 1771, Boone explored the area with five other men. His family stayed behind in North Carolina the entire time. Trying to find a way across the high mountains, Boone's party loaded their packhorses with rifles, powder, animal traps, bedding, lead for making bullets, and kettles for cooking. They headed west through the Blue Ridge, which was part of the Appalachian Mountain range. Then they made their way to the Warrior's Path, a trail through hills and valleys that Native Americans had used for years. This brought them to a set of cliffs called the White Rocks, where they found a gap in the mountains. Although it was narrow, it allowed Boone and his party to cross the mountain barrier. The narrow path through the mountains was called the Cumberland Gap.

Boone and his friends did not discover the Cumberland Gap. It had long been used by Native Americans, of course. A few other American colonists had traveled the path, too. Boone would be the first, however, to lead settlers across the Cumberland Gap. His adventures in Kentucky made the Cumberland Gap famous. In the decades to come, hundreds of thousands of people would follow Boone west through the Cumberland Gap.

Boone's party emerged from the mountain pass and slowly made their way down into the foothills of the Appalachians. There they saw the beautiful rolling country-side stretched out before them. Boone later remembered, "We saw with pleasure the beautiful level of Kentucke [sic]. We found everywhere abundance of wild beasts of every sort, through this vast forest." It had been five weeks of hard travel since leaving North Carolina, but Boone was back in Kentucky. Today, a traveler in an automobile could make the same journey in a day.

The hunting was even better than he had remembered. The forests and meadows offered an abundance of deer, buffalo, and elk. For the next few months, Boone and his companions were very busy. Besides hunting, they had to prepare their animal skins for market. The skins had to be scraped clean, then dried, then folded into packs. The hunters laid these packs on top of elevated wood platforms to keep them out of the reach of prowling wolves, and covered them with buffalo skins. Each pack of animal skins weighed about 250 pounds (113 kilograms). Before long, the hunters had gathered hundreds of dollars' worth of animal skins.

THE CUMBERLAND GAP

The Cumberland Gap was named in 1750 by Dr. Thomas Walker, who was exploring for a Virginia land company. He named it after a British general, the Duke of Cumberland.

The Duke of Cumberland, for whom the Cumberland Gap was named

The Cumberland Gap through the Appalachian Mountains provided an opening to the West.

Daniel Boone continued to hunt as an old man.

* * * *

For eight months they worked undisturbed by Native Americans. Then late in 1769, their luck ran out. A group of Shawnee, believing that Boone had no right to be hunting on their hunting ground, attacked Boone's camp. They warned Boone and the others to leave and not come back. To teach them a lesson, the Shawnee took all the animal skins the hunters had prepared. They also took their horses. Boone and the others were left with just enough supplies to make it back over the mountains to their homes.

Boone wasn't ready to go home, however. One by one, his companions returned home or left, but he stayed in Kentucky. He tried to follow the Shawnee and recapture the supplies they had taken from him, but the Shawnee captured Boone a second time and treated him harshly before he managed to escape.

By the following year, Boone and his brother Squire were the only white hunters left in Kentucky. They hunted for another year together, then in the spring of 1770 Squire returned home to retrieve more supplies. Boone was left alone in the wilds of Kentucky until Squire returned in July 1770. Squire made another round-trip to home and back in the fall of 1770. Then Daniel and Squire returned together in March 1771.

His two years of hunting in Kentucky made Boone eager to return. In fact, he intended to bring his family with him and settle in Kentucky. In 1773, he helped organize a group of about fifty settlers who wanted to make new homes across the mountains in Kentucky. They were the first white people to try to settle there. In September 1773, packing everything they needed onto wagons or the backs of animals, the group left their homes and their families behind in North Carolina. They did not know exactly what to expect in Kentucky, though they knew that the Shawnee and other Native American groups would not be happy to see them.

Disaster struck before they even made it over the mountains. A group of Delaware Indians attacked the settlers, killing six of them. Among the dead was Boone's

Delaware Indians are shown here returning English captives. The Delaware were one of the Native American tribes opposed to the settlers' westward expansion.

* * * *

As a captain of the Virginia militia, Boone led the defense against Shawnee attacks.

oldest son, James. The settlers turned back home, and the Boones made a temporary home in Virginia. The first attempt to settle Kentucky had failed.

That attack was just part of the Native Americans' effort to keep white settlers east of the mountains. As the attacks continued into 1774, settlers joined forces to strike back. Boone was made a captain in the Virginia militia and led the defense of his home neighborhood in the war against the Shawnee people. After months of fighting, the Virginia militia defeated the Shawnee. The Virginians forced the Shawnee to sign a peace treaty in which they gave up their claims to Kentucky. In 1775, the Cherokee signed over their rights to Kentucky as well. The way seemed to be clear for another effort to settle that land.

CUTTING THE WILDERNESS ROAD

In the spring of 1775, Boone led a team that set out to cut a two-hundred mile (320 kilometer) road from Virginia to Kentucky. The road snaked through dense wilderness and included narrow mountain paths. It was called the Wilderness Road. Building it was slow and exhausting work. Trees had to be

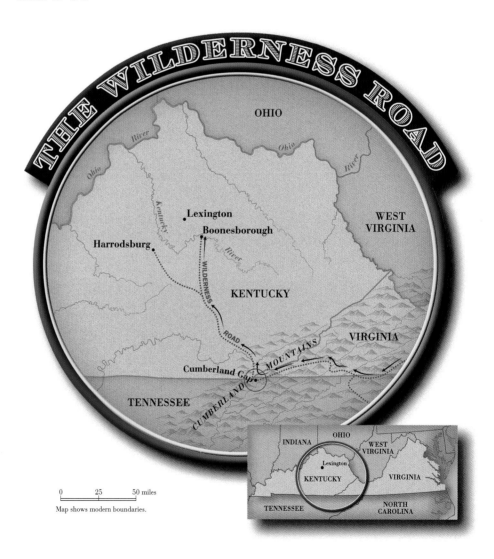

THE WILDERNESS ROAD

OHIO

Ohio River

Ohio River

WEST VIRGINIA

Kentucky River

Lexington

Boonesborough

Harrodsburg

WILDERNESS

KENTUCKY

River

ROAD

VIRGINIA

MOUNTAINS

Cumberland Gap

CUMBERLAND MOUNTAINS

TENNESSEE

0   25   50 miles

Map shows modern boundaries.

INDIANA   OHIO   WEST VIRGINIA

Lexington

KENTUCKY   VIRGINIA

TENNESSEE   NORTH CAROLINA

chopped down, bushes and vines had to be cleared, and rivers and creeks had to be crossed. Finally, in late March, Boone and his twenty-eight road-builders made their way back into Kentucky. They camped on the banks of the Kentucky River and began building a group of log huts there. They called the place Boonesborough.

At the same time, settlements were springing up elsewhere in Kentucky. By the summer of 1775, hundreds of white settlers were living there. Representatives of the

FOLLOWING BOONE'S TRAIL

Travelers can still follow the route of the Wilderness Road. Today's U.S. Route 25 carries cars over much of the original Wilderness Road.

The Kentucky River

Boone escorted many settlers through the Cumberland Gap.

brand-new towns met in Boonesborough to begin setting up a government. Boone was selected to represent Boonesborough. In September, Rebecca Boone and the rest of the family joined Boone in Kentucky, becoming part of a stream of settlers who made their way to Kentucky in 1775 and 1776. As Boonesborough began to grow, the circle of log huts became a fort. Families began building houses with wooden floors and glass windows. Still, they lived in danger.

In the summer of 1776, Boone's thirteen-year-old daughter, Jemima, and two of her friends were kidnapped by a group of Cherokee and Shawnee. The girls had taken a **canoe** out on the Kentucky River in order to gather wild grapes. When they wandered too far from the fort, five Native Americans quickly grabbed the canoe. The girls

Canoes were important for river travel for both settlers and Native Americans.

screamed for their lives. Their screams alerted the people of Boonesborough. The Native Americans made off into the woods with their new captives. Boone and four others quickly followed.

As their captors led them along, the girls tried to leave a trail for their rescuers, breaking off tree branches or pulling up vines. Boone and his men tracked them for two days. They caught up to them when the Native Americans made camp on the second night. Boone and the others surrounded the Native American camp and waited for their chance to strike. Concealed in the woods, the skilled riflemen took aim and

31

made sure not to fire toward the girls. Their first volley wounded several Native Americans. The rest of them fled into the woods. Meanwhile, the frightened girls hurried toward their rescuers. In the dim light of the forest, one of the settlers mistook one of the girls for a Native American. As she ran toward him, he raised his rifle to defend himself. Alarmed, Boone shouted, "For God's sake, don't kill her when we've traveled so far to save her."

An artist's rendering of the capture of Jemima Boone and her two friends

This is a depiction of the captured girls being rescued

Exhausted and relieved, Boone and the girls exchanged hugs and collapsed. "Let's all sit down now and have a hearty cry," Boone told them all. The group returned to Boonesborough without encountering the Native Americans again. Back at the settlement, there were more hugs, more tears, and more rejoicing as the townspeople celebrated the safe return of the girls.

Conflict with Native Americans in Kentucky was just beginning. That same summer the Americans declared their independence from Great Britain. In August 1776, a messenger arrived in Boonesborough with a copy of the

Declaration of Independence. He read it aloud to the towns-people, who celebrated around a bonfire that night. The American Revolution soon reached Kentucky when the British urged their Indian allies to strike American frontier settlements. Boone had organized the men of Boonesborough into a militia unit to defend the town. He had also arranged for several hundred pounds of gunpowder and bullets to be sent to the town from Virginia. In April 1777, Shawnee warriors attacked Boonesborough. They caught

Boonesborough, Kentucky, was one of the two settlements, along with Boone's Station, that Daniel Boone founded in Kentucky. Notice how each log cabin makes up part of the wall of the fort.

* * * *

two townsmen outside the gates of the fort and killed one of them. Boone and twelve more settlers charged out of the fort at the Shawnee, firing their rifles and swinging them like clubs. Boone was wounded by a bullet in the ankle and fell to the ground in severe pain. One of the Shawnee jumped on top of Boone with a tomahawk and was about to kill him, but a settler named Simon Kenton came to his rescue. Kenton fought off the Shawnee warrior and dragged the wounded Boone back into the fort. Eventually all of the settlers were able to drive off the Shawnee and reach the safety of the fort. In addition to the one settler killed, four others were wounded.

DEFENDING BOONESBOROUGH

During the siege of Boonesborough, the defenders of the fort made squirt guns out of old rifle barrels and then used them to put out fires started by flaming Indian arrows.

The Shawnee continued to raid American frontier settlements in Kentucky. They burned the settlers' cornfields and made it impossible for farmers to plant or harvest their crops. As a result, the food supply in Boonesborough and other settlements came dangerously close to running out. The Shawnee attacks also made it dangerous for settlers to venture out to gather salt.

Salt was a necessity for people on the frontier. They used it to preserve the meat that hunters brought in, so that it could be kept for long periods of time. Salt also made the settlers' vegetables and cornmeal easier to consume. Without salt, hunters would have to head out every few days or so to bring in fresh meat. To produce salt, frontiersmen gathered underground water that had been made salty by minerals beneath the earth's surface. This salty water bubbled to the surface at salt springs. The settlers

35

boiled the water down in large kettles until nothing was left but salt, then scraped the salt off the sides of the kettle. It was extremely difficult work, requiring teams of workers to gather wood for fuel, tend the fires, and pack the salt. It took about five hundred gallons of water to produce a fifty-pound load of salt.

In January 1778, Boone led a party of armed men many miles to the north of Boonesborough to harvest salt. While the harvesting continued, Boone went out on his own one day to hunt, and was captured by four Shawnee warriors. The warriors were part of a larger group under the command of the Shawnee leader Blackfish, who had been attacking frontier settlements. Boone was led away to a Shawnee village on the other side of the Ohio River, where he met Blackfish.

Blackfish told Boone that he planned to attack Boonesborough and kill all the settlers. Boone convinced Blackfish to let him lead the Shawnee to the town in the spring, when he would arrange for its peaceful surrender. Boone also surrendered the twenty-seven other members of the salt-making party to the Shawnee. All the men were led away to be adopted into Shawnee families. It was a common practice among the Shawnee to adopt enemy prisoners to replace other family members lost in war. The prisoners had to endure a painful adoption ceremony that included having most of their hair plucked from their head. Blackfish himself came to admire Boone and adopted him into his family. He named Boone "Big Turtle."

The Battle of the Blue Licks helped end Native American help for the British.

Boone lived with the Shawnee for six months. The twenty-seven others were sold for a bounty. Finally, fearing that the Shawnee would soon attack Boonesborough, Boone decided to try to escape and warn the town. He slipped away from the Shawnee village on horseback, taking only a little bit of preserved meat, a broken rifle, and some ammunition. Knowing that the Shawnee would be in pursuit, he rode as fast as he could until his horse tired. He then continued on foot, running through streams and over fallen trees to hide his trail. He covered 150 miles in four days. On June 20, 1778, he returned to

Boonesborough. His wife and most of his children, fearing that he had been killed, had returned to North Carolina. Only his daughter Jemima was still in Boonesborough, waiting patiently for his return.

When the Shawnee attack came in September, Boone again led the defense. This time, the Shawnee laid **siege** to the town for eleven days. They charged the fort and tried to set fire to it. They even tried to tunnel under the fort's walls. When nothing worked, the Shawnee finally gave up their siege.

Warfare with the Shawnee raged for years. Boone took part in an attack on the Shawnee in 1780. In 1782, his son Israel was killed in a battle with an army of Shawnee supported by the British. The conflict was called the Battle of Blue Licks, one of the last battles fought during the American Revolution. The next year the war between Great Britain and the new United States of America ended. Without the help of the British, the Shawnee and other Native American tribes were forced to move north.

THE LEGEND GROWS

As Kentucky grew, Boone became one of its leaders. He was elected to the Virginia State Assembly in 1780, when Kentucky was still part of Virginia. He served there on and off for much of the 1780s and 1790s. He also was promoted to colonel in the county militia. Stories of his adventures spread all over the United States. In 1784, a writer named John Filson published *The Adventures of Colonel Daniel Boon* [sic]. Filson's book helped make Boone famous in his own lifetime.

Despite Daniel Boone's many accomplishments, he was still not ready to settle down. He kept moving from place to place. In 1779, he started a new settlement at Boone's Station in Kentucky. In 1783, he moved his family to the town of Limestone, on the Ohio River, and later

BOONE'S BIOGRAPHER

Like Daniel Boone, John Filson was born in Pennsylvania and moved to Kentucky. He was a schoolteacher there when he wrote the book that made Boone famous.

The Ohio River became an important highway for western settlement.

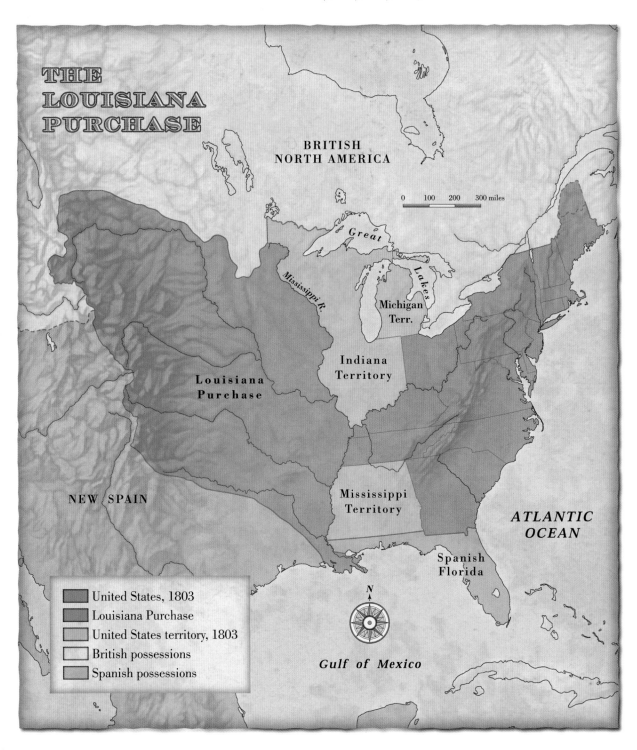

THE LOUISIANA PURCHASE

BRITISH NORTH AMERICA

0   100   200   300 miles

Great Lakes

Mississippi R.

Michigan Terr.

Indiana Territory

Louisiana Purchase

NEW SPAIN

Mississippi Territory

ATLANTIC OCEAN

Spanish Florida

N

United States, 1803
Louisiana Purchase
United States territory, 1803
British possessions
Spanish possessions

Gulf of Mexico

to present-day West Virginia. In 1795, he returned to Kentucky. In 1799, he made one last move. This time he moved out of the United States.

He led his family to a new home in present-day Missouri, where his son Daniel Morgan Boone had found beautiful land. The soil was rich and the game was plentiful. At the time, much of the land west of the Mississippi River was controlled by Spain. Spanish leaders were glad to have the famous Daniel Boone in their territory. In 1799, the Spanish made Boone a "syndic," or local leader. He acted as a frontier judge, settling disputes among neighbors. Most important to Boone, however, was that he had plenty of room to hunt and trap.

THE LOUISIANA PURCHASE

The area that Boone moved to in Missouri was part of the immense territory that the United States bought in 1803. Called the Louisiana Purchase, the deal doubled the size of the United States.

President Thomas Jefferson purchased the Louisiana Territory from France.

The monument to Daniel and Rebecca Boone, erected in Frankfort Cemetery in 1862 by the state of Kentucky

★ ★ ★ ★

As time passed, Boone wasn't able to hunt the way he used to. As he grew older, his health was not as good. He suffered from stiff joints—the result of years of sleeping in damp woods. His eyesight began to fail, too.

Rebecca Boone died in 1813. Deeply saddened by the loss of his wife, Boone began preparing for his own death. Seven years later, on September 26, 1820, Daniel Boone died at eighty-five years of age, surrounded by family and friends.

Boone spent most of his life leading the way west for other settlers. Like so many Americans throughout the nation's history, he bravely moved to new lands in search of a better life for his family. Like the young United States itself, Boone kept pushing westward. When he was born in Pennsylvania in 1734, the United States didn't even exist. When he died in Missouri eighty-five years later, the United States was a growing country that stretched from the Atlantic Ocean to territories on the Pacific coast. The United States kept growing because of the restless spirit of trailblazers like Daniel Boone.

A portrait of Daniel Boone toward the end of his life

Glossary

breechclout—strip of cloth that hung from a belt and was folded between the legs

canoe—a light, narrow boat that is moved by paddling

game—wild animals that are hunted for food

herdsman—a keeper of a herd of animals

livestock—horses, cattle, sheep, and other animals kept on a farm

pelts—the skins or furs of wild animals

persecution—suffering inflicted on people by authority because of their beliefs

settlers—people who move to and live in a new land

siege—a long battle staged to capture or defeat a fort or city

trailblazers—people who find or make roads or paths for others to follow

weaver—a person who makes fabric or cloth

Timeline: Daniel Boone

1734	1751	1756	1767	1769	1775	1776
Daniel Boone is born on October 22.	Boone family settles in western North Carolina.	Daniel Boone marries Rebecca Bryan on August 14.	Boone hunts in Kentucky for the first time.	Boone begins two-year hunting and exploring trip in Kentucky.	Boone family settles in Kentucky.	Boone and others rescue Jemima Boone and two other girls kidnapped by the Shawnee.

and the Cumberland Gap

1778	1781	1784	1799	1813	1820	Today
Boone is captured by the Shawnee. He escapes and leads the defense at the siege of Boones- borough.	Boone is elected to the Virginia Assembly for the first time.	*The Adventures of Colonel Daniel Boon* [sic] is published.	Boone moves to Missouri and is appointed "syndic."	Rebecca Boone dies on March 18.	Daniel Boone dies on September 26.	Route 25 follows the path of Boone's Wilderness Road

To Find Out More

BOOKS

Calvert, Patricia. *Daniel Boone: Beyond the Mountains.* Tarrytown, NY: Benchmark Books, 2001.

Kozar, Richard. *Daniel Boone and the Exploration of the Frontier.* Broomall, PA: Chelsea House, 2000.

McCarthy, Pat. *Daniel Boone: Frontier Legend.* Berkeley Heights, NJ: Enslow, 2000.

ONLINE SITES

Fort Boonesborough State Park
http://www.state.ky.us/agencies/parks/ftboones.htm

Daniel Boone Homestead
http://www.berksweb.com/boone.html

Archiving Early America
http://earlyamerica.com/lives/boone/index.html

Index

Bold numbers indicate illustrations.

About the Author

Andrew Santella writes for magazines and newspapers, including *Gentlemen's Quarterly* and the *New York Times Book Review*. He is the author of several Children's Press books, including *The Assassination of Robert F. Kennedy* and *Mount Rushmore*.